Introducing

Fun for One

Do you ever wonder what to do when you are on your own? Here are lots of new ways to amuse yourself.

Perhaps you are lying in bed – perhaps you have to wait for a bus – perhaps you have a whole day to fill. Here are games for a few moments and games for a long wet afternoon and games to play over a longer period.

Have fun wherever you are.

Also by Deborah Manley

The Dragon Seaside Book

Deborah Manley

Fun for One

DRAGON
GRANADA PUBLISHING
London Toronto Sydney New York

Published by Granada Publishing Limited
in Dragon Books 1979

ISBN 0 583 30293 9

A Dragon Original
Copyright © Deborah Manley 1979

Granada Publishing Limited
Frogmore, St Albans, Herts AL2 2NF
and
3 Upper James Street, London W1R 4BP
1221 Avenue of the Americas, New York, NY 10020, USA
117 York Street, Sydney, NSW 2000, Australia
100 Skyway Avenue, Toronto, Ontario, Canada M9W 3A6
110 Northpark Centre, 2193 Johannesburg, South Africa
CML Centre, Queen & Wyndham, Auckland 1, New Zealand

Set, printed and bound in Great Britain by
Cox & Wyman Ltd., London, Reading and Fakenham
Set in Intertype Times

Granada Publishing ®

Contents

Acknowledgments

The lines from *Paper Boats* by Rabindranath Tagore are
reprinted from *The Collected Poems and Plays of Rabindranath Tagore* by permission of the Trustees of the Tagore
Estate, and Macmillan London and Basingstoke.

Arithmetic by Carl Sandburg is reprinted from *Complete
Poems* by Carl Sandburg by permission of Harcourt Brace
Jovanovich, Inc. Copyright © 1950, Carl Sandburg.

Ounce to Denim, Instant to Dentist, Archery to Dennity
are all reprinted from *Ounce, Dice Trice* by Alastair Reid,
published by J. M. Dent & Sons Ltd, by kind permission
of Laurence Pollinger Limited.

It has proved impossible to locate the copyright holder of
Verbs by Dele Olanyi. We have printed the poem and hope
that the author or copyright holder will get in touch with us.

Outdoors

SWINGING

One of the best of all things to do on your own is to swing.
You must, of course, make sure that your swing is entirely
safe, so it should either be one that is bought or one made by
a grown up. If your swing is to be hung from a tree, someone
will have to check that the branch is really strong and safe.

You can make a swing, too, from a rubber tyre, like this:

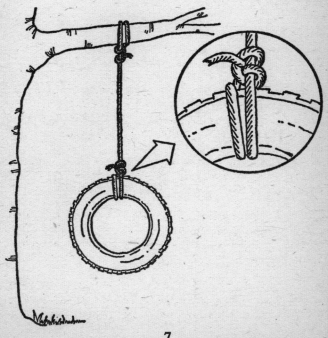

The Swing

How do you like to go up in a swing,
   Up in the air so blue?
Oh, I do think it the pleasantest thing
   Ever a child can do!

Up in the air and over the wall,
   Till I can see so wide,
Rivers and trees and cattle and all
   Over the countryside –

Till I look down on the garden green,
   Down on the roof so brown –
Up in the air I go flying again,
   Up in the air and down!

                    Robert Louis Stevenson

Of course you can play hopscotch competing against other people, but it's a good game to play by yourself too.

All you need is a bit of chalk, a place to draw your frame (like a piece of concrete or a pavement which is not too well used by other people) and a pebble.

The basic principle of hopscotch is that you throw the stone into each of the squares of your frame in order, hop up and down the frame, missing the square where your pebble is, then pick up the stone on the return journey, again missing that square as you hop out of the frame.

Here are some of the different frames you can use in hopscotch:

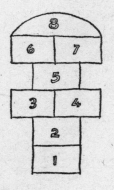 

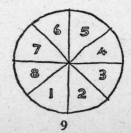

FIVE STONES

This game was once played with little pieces of mutton bone and called Knucklebones. You can use any smooth little stones you pick up from the ground, or jacks or special sets of five stones bought in a shop. The ancient Greeks used to play it and it is now played as far away as Japan.

You can play five stones on a table, but it is much better to play it squatting on the ground or on a wood or lino floor.

There are many different throws to work through and you will probably invent more of your own. But here's how to begin. Cast four of the stones upon the ground. Throw the fifth stone into the air and pick up one of the four stones on the ground before you catch the first stone in the same hand.

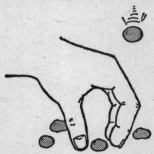

Put the picked up stone to one side, then throw the first one again, picking up another stone. Continue in this way until you have picked up all the stones. Now throw the first stone up in the air and pick up all four other stones together in the same hand.

Here are some of the variations to this game.

1 Throw up the first stone and pick up the other stones in pairs.
2 Throw up the first stone, pick up the others one at a time, as in the first game, but catch the first stone on the back of your hand.
3 Hold all the stones in your hand. Throw up one and put another down on the floor before catching the one you threw up. Get all the stones on to the floor in this way. Then throw up the first stone and pick them all up again.

4 Put the four stones in a line on the floor. Pick up the first and third stone at the first throw and the second and fourth stone at the second throw.

5 Under the arch: Put one hand on the ground so that the thumb and index finger form an arch. With your other hand throw down the stones in front of it. Pick up one to use as the 'jack', throw it up and then knock the stones one at a time through or towards the arch. In later turns you knock two stones at a time, then three and one and then all four through the arch.

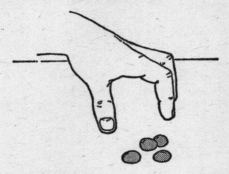

6 The stable doors: Spread your hand out on the ground, fingers apart, palm lifted. The gaps between your fingers and between your index finger and your thumb are the four 'stable doors'. Throw your stones in front of the stable. Pick up your 'jack'. Now, while you throw up the jack, knock a stone into each of the stable doors in turn. Continue to play until all the 'stables' are full.

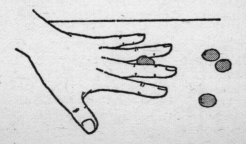

SEVENS

When we were schoolchildren in Canada we used to play this game for hours both in school break time and at home. You can play it with people taking turns but, on your own, you don't have to wait for anybody.

All you need is a ball the size of a tennis ball and a wall with some hard bouncing space in front of it. We used to use special very hard rubber balls. I think they were probably lacrosse balls and would be quite expensive to buy. But they certainly bounced beautifully. An ordinary tennis ball or rubber ball will do, of course.

The game consists of throwing the ball against the wall in seven different ways and in any number of different styles. If you fail to catch it you have to go back to the beginning of the group of seven and start again. Once you get really adept you may challenge yourself to work through several styles without missing a catch and return to the start of the whole series if you do miss.

Here are the seven throws:

1 Throw the ball against the wall and catch it without it bouncing.
2 Throw the ball and let it bounce once before you catch it.
3 Throw the ball under your leg against the wall and catch it without it bouncing.

4 Throw the ball on the ground so that it bounces up against the wall and catch it without it bouncing.

5 Throw the ball, let it bounce, bounce it on the ground, throw it up again and catch it before it bounces.
6 Throw up the ball and catch it without it bouncing as in the first throw.
7 Throw up the ball, let it bounce while you spin round once before catching it.

Here are some of the different styles you can use to play each group of seven throws:
1 Catch with both hands.
2 Catch with the right hand only.
3 Catch with the left hand only.
4 Clap your hands together before you catch the ball.
5 Spin round on each throw and twice on throw seven.
6 Play the series down on one knee.
7 Use styles four to six using the right or left hand only.

You can invent new styles for yourself, but you will find getting through this series without a drop will be quite an achievement!

You can have great fun in the garden (or even indoors if you have a large enough room) making and playing on your own crazy golf course. I once saw one in Italy which had been laid out permanently with concrete lanes edging little flower beds as part of a garden.

You need to plan and lay out your course carefully, thinking out the various obstacles you can make. Use the natural contours of the land (the mounds and valleys of the ground) and any materials available. See how many shots you need to get round your course using a putting club if you have one, or make one by nailing a piece of wood at right angles to a straight stick. Use an ordinary golf or other small ball.

Add to your course whenever you get a new idea and change it round to create variation. Here are a few ideas to get you started.

Collect together as many of these things as you can to make your obstacles: cardboard cartons and large sheets of card, empty squeezy bottles, a cardboard roll large enough for the ball to pass through, an old baking tin, yoghurt cups, sticks. You will also need a strong pair of scissors and a knife. You can also cut sheets of card from the sides of some of the cardboard boxes. Make a slope by standing the end of a card on yoghurt cups.

Lay the long roll on its side. Set out the squeezy bottles to make an awkward hazard and build slopes into and out of the baking tray.

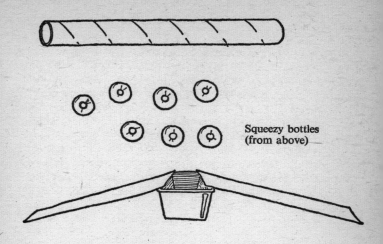

Squeezy bottles
(from above)

Cut out the ends of three shoe boxes and set them in line with the central one slightly raised:

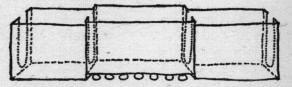

Cut arches through larger cardboard boxes; lay out a narrow alley bordered by sticks.

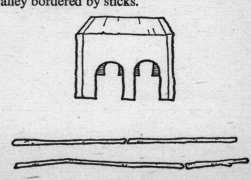

Flying a kite is a wonderful experience. I have stood with my father on the cliffs above the Suffolk sea shore with our kites fluttering high above us, pulling at their lines, their tails sashaying out behind them whipped by the wind from the North Sea.

People have flown kites for at least two thousand years, ever since the Chinese, probably the most famous of all kite flyers, sent their silk and bamboo kites high into the air. Kites have been used in war and for scientific research; kites have been flown in competitions and to make weather observations. But mostly they are flown just for the sheer fun of it.

Kites come in all different shapes – from the complex shapes of box kites to the natural shapes of birds, butterflies and fish. I'm going to tell you how to make one of the most simple shapes: the diamond.

You will need:

Two light pieces of wood. To get the proportions of your kite right the longer piece for the spine should be 85 cm (34 in) long; the shorter crosspiece should be 70 cm (28 in) long.

A piece of strong but light paper or cloth.

Strong thread or fine string.

A penknife or cutting tool and scissors.

Glue, paint and a paint brush.

To make up your kite:

1 Cut a notch across the width of each end of the pieces of the frame. (Later you will tie a piece of string around the frame to fix the paper onto and this string will pass through these notches.)

2 Mark the centre of the crosspiece. Mark a point 20 cm (8 in) from the top of the spine. Join the two pieces together at these points by first lashing them together with string

and then putting a strong adhesive glue over the string to fix it firmly.

3 Now fix a piece of thread through the notches you made at the ends of the frame pieces so that it goes right round the frame. Pull the thread tight and tie the ends together. You have now made the diamond outline of your kite.

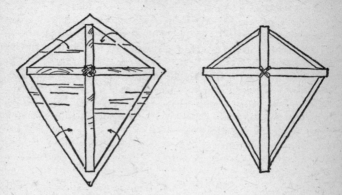

4 Lay the frame down on your paper or cloth and cut a diamond shape 1–2 cm ($\frac{1}{2}$ in) bigger all round than the frame.

5 If you want to paint a pattern on your kite this is the point at which to do it.

6 Now lay the frame on the paper again with the crosspiece down against it. Fold the paper over the diamond-shaped guideline. Cut away the paper where the crosspiece and the spine join the paper so that they stick out beyond it.

7 Glue the folded edges carefully down over the guideline so that the string is fixed inside the fold of the paper.

8 Now the kite itself is ready. But it is not yet ready to fly. It still needs what is called the 'bridle', the string on which the main flying line is fixed (like the bridle to which a horse's reins are attached). Your kite has to have a tail too, which will help to keep it from spinning in the air when you fly it.

17

9 To make the bridle: Tie a length of string at the top and bottom of the spine. Join the two lengths about 25–30 cm (10–12in) from the kite and opposite the place where the spine and crosspiece join.

10 To make the tail: Cut a number of strips of lightish weight cloth or crêpe paper. They should be about 5 cm (2 in) wide and 15 cm (6 in) long. Take a length of string about 4 metres (4 yd) long. Tie the string around the centre of each strip so that the strips hang off it about 10–15 cm (4–6 in) apart. Tie the tail to the bottom of the kite's spine.

11 Now you need a line to fly your kite on. You can buy kite line on a reel in some toy shops. Otherwise you can use fishing line or a stronger thread like buttonhole thread. Tie it to the bridle with a firm knot that will not slip. At last your kite is ready to fly!

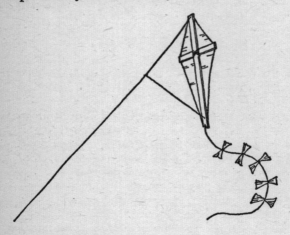

How to fly your kite:
Choose a suitable day: not a *very* windy day and not a *very* calm one. A 'breezy' day is what you want. Stand with your back to the wind. Throw your kite up into the air in front of you. Feed the line out to the kite as fast as it will take it, but not so fast that you are feeding out slack line. Yank the line

so that it lifts the kite upwards. If you walk backwards away from the kite, this will help to lift it as well. If you have a friend with you it may help if she or he takes the kite about 30 metres (or yards) downwind from you and tosses the kite up into the air for you. Kite flying is not quite as simple as that makes it sound! You may find that you have to adjust your kite in various ways: shortening the tail, for instance. And try experimenting with various sorts of pulls and yanks on the string while the kite is flying.

The first kite you make may not, let's face it, be entirely satisfactory. You may think that it is a good idea to buy a cheap cotton or plastic kite with which you can learn kite flying and then make your own kite when you have conquered the basic skills. Or you may, of course, be successful enough with your home made kite to want to make more. If you do want to go on with this there are several books which will help you. Your local library should be able to give you details.

BURIED TREASURE

When my sister and I were children we lived in India. And before we left India we buried a treasure there. Perhaps no one will ever find it hidden away on the top of a rock outcrop. Perhaps some Indian child found it years ago. We will never know. But the memory of burying our treasure is still fresh.

Why don't you bury a treasure? And if you do, what sort of treasure should you bury?

One thing is important – your treasure should contain some information about yourself and about why you are burying it. You can write this in the form of a letter in a sealed envelope, addressed:

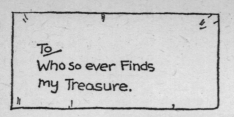

To
Who so ever Finds
my Treasure.

Then bury some things which will tell about the time in which you live. You will need a tin box, such as a biscuit tin, to put them in and a plastic bag or sheet of plastic to keep away damp and decay.

You will probably have plenty of ideas of your own about what you will bury, but here are some to start you thinking:

a photograph of yourself and/or your family

a photograph of your house (perhaps the finder may one day come to look at it)

a postcard of a typical scene in your town

a tenpence piece with a list of the things you can buy with it

some postage stamps on dated envelopes

the front page of a newspaper

Then you could also put in your treasure chest some 'treasures' to please the person who finds it. You probably shouldn't put in anything too precious unless you ask your parents first. But you might put in a few things like these:

a small bottle of scent

a little bar of soap

match folders advertising places in your town

a small toy

a little glass animal or china object

a paperback book

Now your treasure is prepared. Where will you hide it? You could choose your own garden (making sure you are allowed to dig a hole there first!) or a piece of waste ground or somewhere in the countryside. Make a map of where you have buried your treasure and one day you may go back and dig it up yourself. But don't go back too soon! Perhaps you could give the map to your own children when you are grown up so that they can search for and find your treasure.

BY THE WATERSIDE

Here are two things to do if you live by a stream or river or near the sea.

PAPER BOATS

Take a sheet of paper and write a message on it in ballpoint pen, which is reasonably waterproof. Then fold the paper into a boat as shown here. Toss your paper boat into the river and wait to see if anyone ever receives and replies to your message.

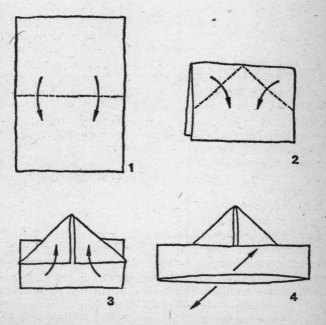

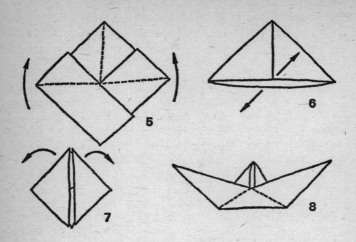

From *Paper Boats*

Day by day I float my paper boats one by one down the
running stream.

In big black letters I write my name on them and the name
of the village where I live.

I hope that someone in some strange land will find them and
know who I am.

I load my little boats with *shiuli* flowers from our garden,
and hope that these blooms of the dawn will be carried
safely to land in the night . . .

Rabindranath Tagore

MESSAGE IN A BOTTLE

When my sister and I came back to England from the time
we spent in Canada, we wrote messages and put them into
tightly corked bottles and threw them over the side of the
ship. I don't know how many we threw, probably a dozen,
but only one was ever found as far as we knew. But the

22

excitement of that find! – both to the person who found it, a German soldier who was working near the beaches of northern Europe, and to us when he wrote.

This is the sort of message you might put in your bottle.

My name is Sarah Collins.
I am throwing this bottle into the sea off the coast of Suffolk, England, on this day, the 23rd May 1976.
Please will you, who have found it, write to me to let me know where you found my message. My address is Blackbird House, White Lane, Redbridge, England.

Where Go the Boats?

> Dark brown is the river,
>   Golden is the sand.
> It flows along for ever,
> With trees on either hand.
>
> Green leaves a-floating,
>   Castles of the foam,
> Boats of mine a-boating –
>   Where will all come home?
>
> On goes the river
>   And out past the mill,
> Away down the valley,
>   Away down the hill.
>
> Away down the river,
>   A hundred miles or more,
> Other little children
>   Shall bring my boats ashore.

Robert Louis Stevenson

COIN GAMES

Coins in a plate

This is a good game for the beach or on a picnic. You need a few coins, but pebbles will do, and a metal or plastic plate. Put the plate on the ground. Stand about three metres or yards back from it and try to throw the coins on to the plate. Unless you are skilful they will skim straight off again! See how many you can get to stay on at one time. Move back further to challenge your own skill.

Coin juggling

These are games which you can try at any time when you have a coin in your pocket. Hold a coin in your hand. Throw it up and try to catch it on the back of your hand. Put a coin on the back of your fingers while they are closed. Open your fingers so that the coin drops through. Catch it as it falls. Now try something rather more skilful. Start by balancing the coin on your elbow. Drop your arm and try to catch the coin in your hand as it falls. Once you have mastered this, try using two or more coins in the same way. How many coins can you work the trick up to?

Pennies in a bucket

Here is a good game from summer fêtes, which is just as frustratingly enjoyable to play on your own. Get a bucket of water, a tenpenny piece and a few twopenny pieces. Drop the tenpenny piece into the bucket. Try to cover it by dropping the twopenny pieces in on top of it one by one.

For this game you need several skittles and a football or large plastic ball. You can get the skittles very easily by collecting empty squeezy bottles from your family and neighbours. If you can't get squeezy bottles quickly enough, see if you can get together a number of soft drink or beer cans. They make good skittles too.

Set up your 'skittles' in a circle about one to two metres away from a wall (vary the distance to give variety to the game). Leave enough room between the skittles for the ball to pass between them without knocking them over.

Now kick the ball up against the wall so that it bounces back into the circle and knocks down some of the skittles. How many skittles can you knock over in one turn?

Indoors

DARTS

If you have a darts board and three darts (or even one), you can play some very satisfactory games against yourself. The practice will also stand you in good stead when you want to challenge other players.

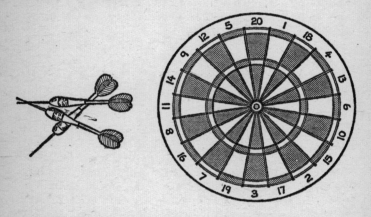

You can score by seeing how many goes you need to complete the game and then in future you can try to improve your own record.

Here are the rules for some games.

301
The aim of this game is to throw your darts to the total of 301. You must start on a double and end on a double. You score from 301 down, like this:

301
    (double 7, 6, 20)

261

(13, double 10, 2)

226

and so on until you reach under 100. Now start going for a score which will allow you to finish on a double. For example, say you have reached 75:

75 (score you want: 35 and double 20)

(score you get: 20, 6, 14)

35 (score you want: 1 and double 17)

Round the clock

For this game you start and finish with a bull's eye. Once you've got your first bull's eye, you have to get a dart in order round the board from 1 to 20 and then put a final dart into the bull again.

PITCH BOARD

This might be called an indoor version of hopscotch. On a sheet of paper or card you draw a form which looks like an irregular brick wall. Number the largest spaces with the lowest number, increasing the scores as the size of the spaces decreases. Collect together a number of pennies to pitch. If you have a game of tiddlywinks or a board game with flat plastic counters, you could borrow these (but make sure you put them back afterwards).

Set yourself a target score, say 100, and pitch the pennies on to the frame from a distance of under a metre. Score only those pennies which fall within a space without crossing any lines. Once you have reached 100 play the next game from further back so that you increase your skill. How long is the shortest time in which you can reach your target score?

MARBLE BOWLING

To make this game you need a piece of stiff cardboard about 25–30 cm long and 8 cm high and another, smaller piece. Cut seven or more arches in the larger card (depending upon how long it is) each not more than 3 cm across. Cut two right angle triangles out of the smaller card, fold them along one edge and glue them firmly to the back of the arched card so that it stands up.

Write a score above each arch. The lowest scores should be at the centre and the highest scores should be at the ends. Can you see why this is? Now, using five marbles and squatting about one metre away from the board, how high a score can you make in one turn?

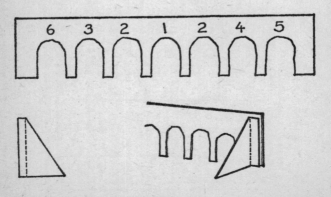

PINGPONG TARGETS

For this game you need a number of small balls, like ping-pong balls, and an equal number of containers, like jam jars, small bowls, cups and boxes. Set the containers out on the ground. Stand back about 2–3 metres or yards and try to throw or bounce one ball into each container.

CUP AND BALL

This toy was played with by children way back in the middle ages, and every generation of children ever since has played versions of it. The simplest way is to have a handle with a cup set on the top of it and a ball tied to the handle with a string. Another version has a ball with a hole in it and a spike instead of a cup on the handle.

You play by holding the cup out in front of you by the handle with the ball hanging down. Then you swing your arm so that the ball flies up and you catch it in the cup (or on the spike).

You can make yourself a similar game with a stick or rod and a wooden or large metal curtain ring. Cut a notch around the centre of the rod. Tie a length of string or fine rope around the notch. This will stop the string from sliding up and down on the rod. Tie the other end of the string through the hook on the ring. Now try to throw the ring over the stick.

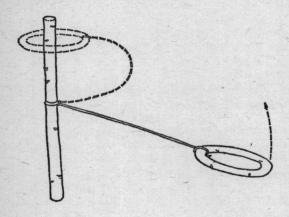

SOLITAIRE DOMINOES

There are a number of games of dominoes which you can play on your own. Some of them are straight adaptations of the games you play with other people, some of them are especially devised for the single player.

First let me explain the basic rules of dominoes. There are 28 dominoes in a *set*. Each domino is divided into two *ends* on which are marked their value in *pips*. Some dominoes have blank ends and there is a double blank in the set. Domino games are played by putting ends with matching pips together. Double ended dominoes are often played across the other dominoes, like this:

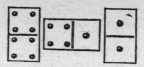

When you are playing a game in which not all the dominoes are used, the pieces which are left over form what is called the *boneyard*. Dominoes were once made from pieces of bone, so that's how this name came about. In some games you also have a *discard pile*, where you put dominoes which have been discarded from the play.

First Game Patience

The game which most players start by learning is called, understandably, the First Game. This solo game is rather similar to that, except that you are playing against yourself rather than against an opponent. Place all the dominoes face down on the table; draw five dominoes from them. The aim of the game is to get all your dominoes down on to the table by matching their ends. Put down one of your dominoes and match one end with another from your hand. Continue to play on to either end until you have played all your dominoes or you have not got one which will match. In that case, draw a domino from the boneyard and go on drawing until you get one which you can play. You now have to play on until you can get all the dominoes in your hand down on to the table. Sometimes you will find that you have turned over all the dominoes from the boneyard and you're still blocked. Many times you will, of course, win!

Side by Side or One over Two

In this game you start with all the dominoes face downward in the boneyard. Turn the dominoes over one by one and lay them side by side in a line, like this:

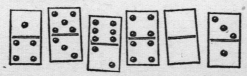

If two dominoes which are side by side have matching pips on them, you discard them and move the line together to close the gap. If dominoes which are two spaces away from each other have the same pips on them, you also discard them and close up the line. In the line above therefore you would discard dominoes 1 and 4, close up the line and then be able to discard dominoes 2 and 6. Of course, as you are playing and discarding as you go, you would not normally have placed all the dominoes as they are in the picture, unless you hadn't noticed that 1 and 4 could be discarded. The aim of the game is to be able to discard all the dominoes. See how close you can get.

A more difficult version of the same game, and one in which there must be absolutely no 'cheating', is to discard only those dominoes which you have placed so that the adjoining ends match. So in the line below you could discard 1 and 2, but not 3 and 4.

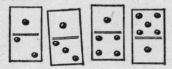

Dozens

The aim of this game is to discard any pairs of dominoes on the table on which the pips add up to a dozen, that is twelve. Start by laying six dominoes face up on the table. If any two dominoes have twelve pips between them, discard both of them. Replace them with dominoes from the boneyard. Continue to discard in this way for as long as you can. If you were lucky enough to turn up the following six dominoes at the first go you would be able to discard them all and replace them from the boneyard. This sort of hand doesn't turn up very often!

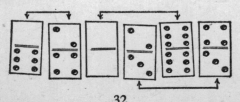

32

Patience games are card games played by one person. Instead of competing against someone else and trying to get the highest score, as you do in many card games, here you compete against the fall of the cards in the pack and your own skill in placing them in an order which will help you to win. Many patience games are pure luck depending on how the cards come out of the pack. Some of them require some skill in positioning cards so that they will be ready when you want to play them on to the table.

Pairs

Deal out twelve piles of three cards each face down on the table. Deal one card face up on each pile. Lay aside the four remaining cards. Now discard any pairs which are face up on the piles. Turn up the next card. Continue to discard any pairs which are turned upwards and turn up the cards beneath. When you have discarded all the cards in any of the four piles, fill the empty space with one of the four extra cards.

You win if you manage to discard the whole pack of cards.

Seven Up

For this game you need to know your seven times table. If you do, you'll probably win almost every time.

Before you start remember that in this game the Jacks count as 11, the Queens as 12 and the Kings as 13.

Play the cards one at a time face upwards in a row. If you deal a 7 you discard it. If the pips on any two or more cards next to each other on the table add up to 7 or a multiple of 7 (that is, 14, 21, 28, 35, etc) you discard them all. Your aim is to discard all the cards in the pack.

Here is an example of how a game might start.

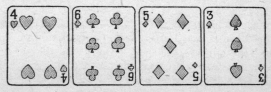

Now, $6 + 5 + 3 = 14 = 2 \times 7$, so you would discard three cards. Your next card might be 7 of Diamonds so you discard it straight away. The next card might be 10 of Hearts. So now you have $4 + 10 = 14 = 2 \times 7$. You discard both cards and start again on the table.

Off the table

Remove the four Aces from the pack and place them face upwards on the table. The aim of the game is to build up suits on these four cards up to King. Deal twenty cards in four rows of five cards each face upwards. Now turn over the stock one card at a time. You can only play from the top card of the waste pile or from the twenty cards in the layout. When you play a card from the layout, fill the space from the waste pile or, if there are no cards there, from the stock.

Can you get all the cards stacked up in sequence?

From the four corners

Take out the four Aces and place them in a square at the centre of the table. Then build up in sequence on these cards in colour (not necessarily in suit) up to the King.

Play from the stock one card at a time. If you can't play direct on to the Aces, play on to four waste heaps which you place at the four corners of the square. Try to place your cards on the waste heaps in descending order (King downwards) so that they will come off the waste heaps in order. If you can't complete the sequences on the first deal, you may pick up the four waste heaps in any order and deal them out once more without shuffling them. This is a game where skill in placing the waste heaps really helps.

The Red and the Black

Remove the two black Aces and the two red Kings from the pack. Lay them face upwards on the table. The aim of the game is to build *upwards* on the Aces and *downwards* on the Kings in *alternate* colours. Deal the pack one at a time. A card goes straight on to the layout if it can. If not you start making four waste piles. You can discard on to these in any way you wish.

The cards on the tops of the waste piles can be played on to the table whenever you need them. The real skill of this game is in the way you build and use your waste piles. When you have dealt the pack once, pick up the waste piles in any order you wish. Without shuffling the pack, deal them again in the same way. You have to get all the cards off the waste piles and on to the table in order this time to win.

Castles in Spain

Deal a row of five cards face down, with a row of four cards above it, a row of three above that and finish off with one card to form a triangle – or castle. Deal two further cards on to each card in the castle, face downwards. Then deal thirteen cards on to the castle face upwards, like this:

The aim of this game is to remove the Aces from the castle and build up on them in suit order to the King.

You may play cards in descending order of alternate colours (red and black) from one pile in the castle to another. You may transfer a full sequence of cards or part of it from one pile to another. When an Ace is turned up you play it out on to the table and start building on it from the castle. Whenever the upturned cards are removed from a

35

pile, you turn over the card beneath and bring it into play. When a pile is removed you can play any sequence or part sequence into that space.

Off the Bottom
Deal six columns of eight cards each, face up. Overlap them top to bottom as shown. If any two cards of the same value are dealt into a column, put the second one to the bottom of the pack and deal the next card. This will give you six columns with eight cards of different values in each. Lay the four spare cards on the table face up.

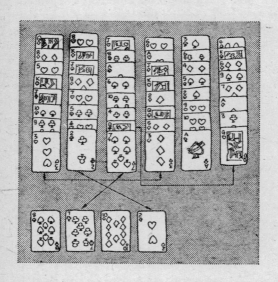

The aim of the game is to pair cards from the bottom of each column and take them away. If the game is blocked, you can pair from the bottom of any column with one of the spare cards.

You can pick up the cards from the six columns (but not the spares which remain on the table until used) shuffle and redeal them twice in order to get the game out.

Labyrinth

This game gets its name from the appearance of the cards on the table during play. This is thought to look like a 'labyrinth' – a network of winding paths through which it is difficult to find one's way.

Take the four Aces out of the pack and set them on the table. The aim of the game is to build up on these four 'foundations' in suit up to King.

Now deal a row of eight cards. Play from these cards on to the Aces if you can. Fill any spaces this play creates. Continue to play from and fill up this row as long as you can.

Then deal out another row of eight cards. Play on to the foundation packs from these cards and from the top row. You can fill up spaces in the second row, but you can no longer fill spaces in the top row. Continue to deal and play from further rows of eight cards.

You may only play from the 'exposed' cards in the top and bottom rows of the labyrinth. If a card is played from the top row it 'exposes' the card immediately below it. If a card is played from the bottom row, it 'exposes' the card immediately above it.

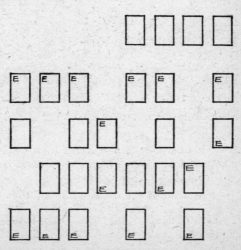

If the play is blocked after dealing a row, you can take one card from any row and play it to a foundation pack.

For this game you are officially only allowed to deal once, but you may like to shuffle and have another deal as it is hard to get it right out!

SHUT THE BOX

This is a very good game to play on your own (although you can play with others). You can buy a set to play with, but if you haven't got one you can make your own very easily out of an empty paper handkerchief box. If you buy a set it will consist of a tray, traditionally lined with green baize with a row of 'boxes' numbered from 1 to 9 along one side. Each box has a sliding top which is moved to cover or reveal the number of the box.

When you play, you start with all the boxes 'open', showing the numbers, and you aim to 'shut' them all with the throws of two dice. I will explain how you do this later. First here's how to make your own version of the game.

All you need is an empty paper handkerchief box, a pair of scissors and a felt-tip pen (or any other writing implement) – and two dice. If the box has an oval opening in it, you will first need to cut this into a longer rectangular opening, like that on some boxes and like the one in the picture. Draw lines on the card at one side of the opening, making nine sections. Cut along these lines so that you have nine flaps along the side of the box. Number the flaps on the underside (what was the inside of the box) from 1 to 9.

Now, if you have your two dice, you are ready to play. Push the flaps up so that all the numbers show. You throw your two dice, into the tray if you have a bought set, or into the box part of your home-made set. You then 'shut the boxes' (push down the flaps so you can't see the numbers) according to your throw, which you can divide or join together as you wish.

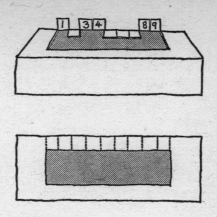

There are two basic methods and you follow one or the other.

1 The Numbers on the Dice You use the numbers on the dice as they appear or as they add up together. For instance, if you throw 5 and 4, you could close either 4 or 5 or you could close 9. Playing this way you are well advised to use the high combined number first.

2 The Sum of the Numbers In this version you can use any combination of the numbers which have made up your throw. For instance if you threw a 3 and a 2, you could use it as 5 or 3 and 2 or 1 and 4. How many ways can you think of dividing a double six so that you could shut as many boxes as possible?

How many turns do you have? Well, again that is up to how you decide to play. You can either have a limited number of throws which you decide beforehand, say six. Or you can continue to throw the dice until you cannot use your throw. For example, say you had shut all the boxes except 4, 5, 6 and you were playing the first version and you threw a double 1, the game would have ended.

Using two dice, which I call A and B in the diagram, see how many different throws can be made to make the numbers 2 to 12. Draw a picture of your answer to help you to check the result. I start the picture for you here to show you what to do and you will be able to check the solution to the puzzle on page 95.

All the Way

If you have two dice there are eleven possible numbers you can throw (although there are, as you have seen from the dice puzzle above, more than eleven ways of throwing them). You can't throw 1 on its own, but you can throw 2, 3, 4, 5, 6, 7, 8, 9, 10, 11, 12. Eleven numbers, as I said.

Now, see how long it takes you to throw all eleven in any order. Then try throwing them in sequence from 2 to 12. Try throwing them in descending order from 12 down to 2. Finally, if you really want to test yourself, try throwing all the combinations which you have worked out as possibilities in the dice puzzle. To do this you really need two dice of different colours, as the A dice and the B dice.

Round the clock dice

This game is rather like Shut the Box. One of the advantages of this version is that, apart from your dice, you need only a pencil and a piece of paper.

For each 'set' you draw a clock face on your paper. You then aim to tick off the 'hours' in order from 1 to 12 by the throw of your dice. You can tick off the hours using either or both dice. For instance, you might throw 5 and 1. You could use this at the start of the game to tick off one o'clock, or, if you threw it later in the game, to cover 5 or 6. If you threw 5 and 6 when you reached that point, you could tick off both hours. Of course, after you pass 6, you have to use both dice to tick off the numbers from 7 to 12.

TIDDLYWINK GAMES

You can buy a tiddlywink game quite cheaply or you can use plastic counters from another game (but be *sure* that you put them back!). You need several small counters and one larger one. For most games you need a target cup or goal. These are usually about 3–5 cm high and about 4 cm across. You could make do with an egg cup, although it will be narrow and therefore make your game more difficult.

The Standard Game
Put the cup on the floor or in the centre of the table. Line your 'winks' up and try to shoot them into the cup by pressing the larger disc, the 'shooter' down on the edge of the wink so that it jumps forward. You can go on shooting the winks from the positions they jump to on the table until you have got them all in the cup. How few shots can you make to achieve your end?

Dangerous ground
Draw a circle around the cup about 25 cm in diameter. Play as for the standard game, except that any winks which fall into the circle must be withdrawn from the game.

Tiddlywink Golf
For this game you have to lay out a course which you shoot your winks around. Lay a cloth out on the floor. A smallish table cloth would be suitable if you are allowed to borrow one. Gather together a number of articles to use as obstacles: crumpled newspaper, books, matchboxes, pieces of wood, toys, pencils, and so on. Collect nine 'cups' which may well be a variety of things from matchbox trays to egg

cups to small saucers and ashtrays. Use these materials to make obstacles between the 'holes' or cups. Put the crumled-up paper under the cloth to make irregularly shaped 'hills'. Build other barriers and hazards as your imagination takes you. Mark flat shooting areas around the course, from which you can aim towards each 'hole'. See how many shots it takes you to get your wink around the course.

FRENCH SOLITAIRE

The traditional solitaire board in France has four more holes and marbles or pegs than the British one, giving the area of play an octagonal shape, like this:

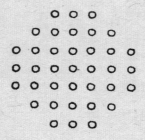

If you know someone who is going to France, you could ask them to get you a French board, or perhaps you are even going there yourself on holiday. You can play a game like the British one on the French board, jumping the marbles and removing them until you have only one marble left on the board.

Another form of this game on the French board is played without all the holes being filled in the first place. In this game the board is like this when you start:

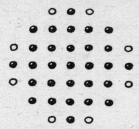

There are some other Solitaire variations which you can play on the French board. Instead of trying to leave only one piece on the board, you aim, by jumping over the pieces, to leave several pieces which form a pattern. Three of the patterns you can work towards are shown below:

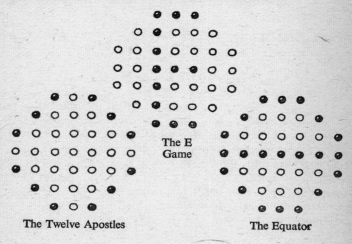

The E Game

The Twelve Apostles

The Equator

The Cross

This last game can be played on either the British or the French board. You start with only nine pieces on the board in the form of a cross:

The aim of the game is to remove eight pieces from the board (by jumping them), leaving only one piece in the middle.

PENNY PUZZLES

Place twelve pennies in six rows so that there are four pennies in each row. See p. 95 for how to do it.

Pass the goats

Three goats coming down a very narrow mountain path meet three goats coming up the path. There is no room for them to pass each other or turn round. But goats can jump and are nimble-footed so they agree to jump over each other one at a time until they have all passed each other. How many jumps must they make?

To help you work out this puzzle put out six pennies like this with one penny or 'goat' space between the two groups. It will make it easier for you if you use 'heads' for the A goats and 'tails' for the B goats. Answer on p. 95.

In Bed

The Land of Counterpane

When I was sick and lay a-bed,
  I had two pillows at my head,
And all my toys beside me lay
  To keep me happy all the day.

And sometimes for an hour or so
  I watched my leaden soldiers go,
With different uniforms and drills,
  Among the bed-clothes, through the hills.

And sometimes sent my ships in fleets
  All up and down among the sheets;
Or brought my trees and houses out,
  And planted cities all about.

I was the giant great and still
  That sits upon the pillow-hill,
And sees before him, dale and plain,
  The pleasant land of counterpane.

Robert Louis Stevenson

Can you say the alphabet backwards without any hesitation or mistakes?

It's much easier to do if you group the letters together, like this:

> Z Y X and W V,
> U T S and R Q P,
> O N M and L K J,
> I H G and F E D
> and C B A.

Alphabetical order

Some people aren't all that good at getting the alphabet in the right order forwards, let alone backwards. You may wonder why it's important. But think of all the things which are listed in alphabetical order and then you will understand.

> telephone directories
> the school register
> the index at the back of a book
> names on a street map
> dictionaries
> encyclopedias
> the gazetteer of an atlas

Can you think of any others?

Do you know how to write things in alphabetical order? It can be more difficult than you think! It's easy enough to list these words in alphabetical order, isn't it?

> DOCTOR   BED   COUGH   ASPIRIN

But what about these?

> PILLOW   PILL   PAIN   PLASTER   PALE

What would you do about those? The answer is that when words begin with the same letter, you have to look at the second letter. But here both PAIN and PALE have A as the second letter. Which goes first? Now you have to look at the third letter. Well, I goes before L in the alphabet, so PAIN goes before PALE in your list. But now you come next to PILL and PILLOW. Here you have to look at the fifth letter before you can decide the order! As PILL has no fifth letter, it goes before PILLOW. But if PILLS was a word in that list where would it go? The answer is after both PILL *and* PILLOW, because S is after O in the alphabet. So now, here's the list in alphabetical order:

> PAIN
> PALE
> PILL
> PILLOW
> PLASTER

Having mastered that, test yourself to see if you can put these two lists of words in alphabetical order. The answer is on page 96.

The answer is on page 96.

THERMOMETER TEMPERATURE TIME TEA
TEST TEN TWENTY TELEPHONE
TELEVISION TOP TRAY TOGETHER

MEASLES MUMPS MANY MARK MASK
MOST MORE MERINGUE MEAT MILK
MAGAZINE MACKEREL MONEY

WORDS FROM A WORD

Have you ever looked for words within a word? You play by choosing a longish word and seeing how many smaller words you can make out of its letters. You may not use each letter more than once in each new word (unless it is repeated in the head word). You may decide to not allow plurals of your words. You can make the game more exciting by setting yourself a time limit of not more than five or ten minutes. It is quite astonishing how many words some people can even find in one minute.

Here is an example showing how many words I managed to get out of the word EXPERIMENTS in five minutes:

exit	rim	ripe	sir	sex	six	in	expert	meet
sire	mine	men	ten	tire	pit	pen	peer
sent	sip	rip	sin	pine	rent	sent	mint
seem	me	spine	stem	pie	spin	mire	rime

That is 33 words.

See how you get on yourself finding words within these words:

TREASURE
SOLITAIRE
KALEIDOSCOPE
CHRISTMAS
REGISTRATION

Can you find more words in five minutes than I did from my word? Choose your own word and try it now. This is a game you can play anytime, anywhere, so long as you have a pen and pencil and a piece of paper.

DOUBLETS

Choose two words with the same number of letters in them. See if you can change one letter at a time in the first word so that you make a new real word but transform it by turns into the second word. Here are some examples of how this can be done.

CART is to be transformed to LIMP
CART CARP CAMP LAMP LIMP

PAGE is to be transformed to FORK
PAGE PARE PARK PORK FORK

Now try these for yourself:
Transform DOGS to CATS
TIME to DAYS

LOGS to FIRE
BOY to MAN
CARD to DICE

SQUARING WORDS

Over a hundred years ago this game was described as an 'agreeable drawing-room game' which 'stimulates the imagination and taxes the knowledge of the player while requiring no special effort'. It can best be explained by giving an example.

You choose a word of from three to six letters, but I suggest that you start with three letters and work up to six. You write this word both vertically and horizontally on a piece of paper. Like this:

D O G
O
G

Now you have to fill in words across and down to form a square of words in each direction, like this:

D O G
O N E
G E T

Here is an example of a six letter square:

C I R C L E
I C A R U S
R A R E S T
C R E A T E
L U S T R E
E S T E E M

You can see there are some hard words in this square so when you are trying to square a six-letter word you are allowed to use two and four-letter or two three-letter words in a line.

MAKING A CROSSWORD PUZZLE

Many people get a lot of fun from doing crosswords. Perhaps you are one of them. But have you ever tried making your own? When you do you will realize how far more difficult it must be to make a really good one than to just do them.

In the usual kind of crossword you have a square which balances itself – and it's the balancing which makes the job most difficult. But here is a simpler sort for you to start with.

Instead of having a square you have a frame which you build on as you go along, like this:

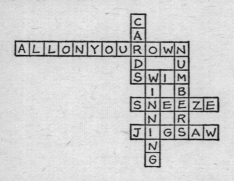

Then you go on building up your frame until you get it as large and complex as you wish. Here is how the frame which began above was completed:

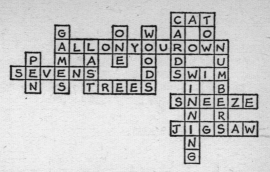

When it is complete you number the head letters of each word regardless of whether they are across or down. Now you are ready to make up the clues. First you do the clues for the words Across and then for the words Down.

Here are some ideas for clues for this frame. I have done the first ten for you. The rest I have mixed up and not numbered so you will need to match and number them yourself. You could then go on and make up different clues which would fit this same frame or start your own crossword with your own clues.

Across 1 I'm the animal which walks by itself.
6 You'll use this book when you are this.
9 One of the games. How many?

Down 1 Jack is one of them
2 To pull behind.
3 Plenty of these in this book.
4 Less than two.
5 Place for a teddy bear's picnic.
7 Play games with them.
8 Use it to write your crossword.

Crawl in water.
Can't see the 5 down for them?
Sign of cold?
Another sort of puzzle.
We all like doing this when we play games.

51

Really the English language can be very difficult! Try reading this old verse devised to include the varieties of pronunciations of the syllable *ough*.

Though the tough cough and hiccough plough me through,
O'er life's dark lough my course I'll pursue.

In those two lines *ough* is pronounced in seven different ways! They are o, uf, of, up, ow, oo and ock.

This poem describes the difficulties a foreigner has in learning English. The author is a Nigerian.

VERBS

A verb is the worst thing in the world,
  For me to learn aright,
And when the teacher calls on me
  I never get it right.

I try to give the parts of verbs
  And say see, saw, seen.
But when I give the parts of be
  I can't say bee, baw, been!

If I give the parts of go
  And say go, went, gone,
It doesn't help a bit with grow!
  I can't say grow, grent, grone.

The parts of take you're very sure
  Are take and took and taken:
Yet bake is very wrong
  As bake and book and baken!

Dele Olanyi

This is game which can be played as a competition between two or more players, but you can play it yourself against the clock. All you need is paper and pencil, a clock or watch – and your wits about you.

Draw a form on your paper like this:

TOPICS			
FLOWER			
COUNTRY			
ANIMAL			
BOY'S NAME			
TREE			

You can choose whichever topics you wish of course. Now pick out three or four letters at random from the page of a book by shutting your eyes and putting your pencil point on to the page anywhere. Where the pencil lands gives you the letter. I chose A, O and D for this form. Then give yourself about five minutes, or however long you think you will need, to see if you can fill in this form. Here is what I was able to do on mine:

TOPICS	A	O	D
FLOWER	Anemone	Orchid	Daffodil
COUNTRY	Austria	—	Denmark
ANIMAL	Anteater	Orangoutang	Dog
BOY'S NAME	Alan	Oliver	Donald
TREE	Alder	Olive	Date palm

Try this quiz for yourself now. How far can you get in five minutes? How much time do you need to complete it?

TOPICS	E	N	H
CITY			
GIRL'S NAME			
BIRD			
FAMOUS PERSON			
FOOD			

MNEMONICS

'What on earth is a mnemonic?' you will probably be asking. It is an aid to memory, that is, a verse or a sentence which helps you to remember the sort of fact which you need from time to time but have often forgotten. You pronounce it 'nemonic'. For some reason mnemonics seem easier to remember than the facts themselves! See if you can learn a few which may stand you in good stead.

Number of days in each month
Thirty days hath September,
April, June and November.
All the rest have thirty-one
Save February alone
Which has twenty-eight days clear
And twenty-nine in each leap year.

The Wives of King Henry VIII
Divorced, beheaded, died;
Divorced, beheaded, survived.

This may, if you know about history, also help you to remember who they were: Catherine of Aragon, Anne

Boleyn, Jane Seymour, Anne of Cleves, Catherine Howard and Catherine Parr.

Metric measurements
To remember the descending order of metric lengths:
>*K*ippers *h*ardly *d*are *m*ove *d*uring *c*old *m*onths.

(Kilometre, Hectometre, Dekametre, Metre, Decimetre, Centimetre, Millimetre)

British Summertime
Do you find it hard to remember which way we put our clocks when we change into and out of summertime?
Spring forward,
Fall back.
(Fall is the North American word for autumn.)

The Order of the Signs of the Zodiac
The Ram, the Bull, the Heavenly Twins,
And next the Crab, the Lion Shines,
The Virgin and the Scales,
The Scorpion, Archer and Sea-Goat,
The Man that bears the watering pot,
And Fish with glittering scales.

Aries, Taurus, Gemini, Cancer, Leo, Virgo, Libra, Scorpio, Sagittarius, Capricorn, Aquarius and Pisces. You will notice that the year of the Zodiac is not the same as our usual year, but starts instead with the month of Aries, 21st March to 19th April.

DESIGNING YOUR MONOGRAM

Have a shot at making a monogram out of the initials of your name. Try different designs to get one which really satisfies you. Use different kinds of letters and different arrangements. Experiment with fitting your initials into a shape like a circle, triangle or diamond. Interleave some flowers and leaves through the letters.

Here are some trial monograms using the initials of my two children, Brett and Adam Manley.

If you make a monogram which really pleases you, you might like to embroider it on your bag or T-shirt or handkerchief, or mark your books with it to identify them.

Here are some ideas for monograms using cross stitch, so that they can be embroidered.

PUT IT TOGETHER AGAIN

Draw a large letter M on card. Cut it out and then cut across the line A–B. You will then have five pieces. See if you can put them all together to make T, F and L. Then, leaving one piece aside, see if you can make an N.

Solution on page 96.

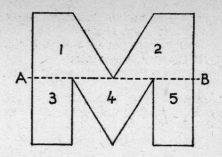

THE MOEBIUS STRIP

Cut a length of paper about five times longer than it is wide. Give one end a half turn and then glue it to the other, so that the strip forms a loop, like this:

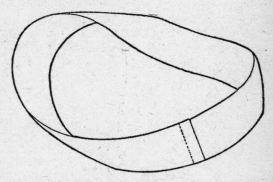

This twisted strip can now provide you with a variety of interesting observations.

1 Starting at any point on the loop, draw a line parallel to the edge which travels right round the loop. What happens?
2 Now cut the loop into two along this line. What happens this time?
3 Cut the loop into two in the same way again, and see what happens.
4 Keep on cutting the loop in two to see what happens.

57

The Tangram is a puzzle which originated in China. It is made from wood, card or even paper cut up into seven pieces and then formed into an enormous number of imaginative shapes.

First you need to make the puzzle. You will need a piece of card about 25 cm (10 in) square. If you can find a piece of black or dark coloured card, so much the better. If not, then colour the card all over on both sides in black or another dark colour. Poster paints would be best for this, but you could use a felt-tip pen or crayons.

Now, using a ruler and pencil, draw a diagonal line across the paper from corner A to corner B. Then lay your ruler from corner C to corner D, but only draw a line half-way, from D to E. Now find the centre of the lines AC and CB. Mark these points, F and G. Join them with a line FG. Continue the line ED to meet line FG at point H. Next find the middle of the line AE. Mark it as point I. Draw the line HI. Then find the middle of the line EB. Mark it at point J. Lastly join G and J to make line GJ.

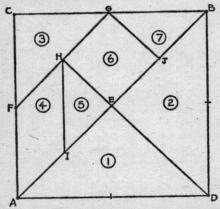

You have now divided the square into seven pieces. Cut along all the lines you have drawn and you have the seven pieces of the Tangram ready to play with.

Here are a few of the patterns you could make with your Tangram pieces. Try these out and then see how many more you can devise. Can you put the square back together again without looking at the book?

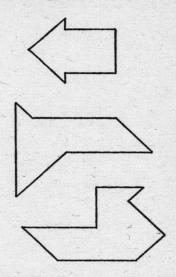

There is more than one way of making a Tangram. When you have exhausted the possibilities of the first one, make yourself this other version.

Again you will need a dark coloured square of card about 25 cm (10 in) square. First you will need to find the exact centre of the square. Do this by measuring 12.5 cm (5 in) along each side and marking these four points. Draw a light line across the square to join these four points E, F, G, H at point I. You are now ready to go ahead with drawing in the main cutting lines.

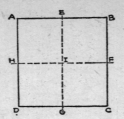

Draw a line from C to I.
Join points D and I.
Join points H and I.
Join points E and I.
Draw a diagonal line to join points E and F.
Find the centres of lines DI and CI. These are points J and K.
Join points J and G and points K and G.

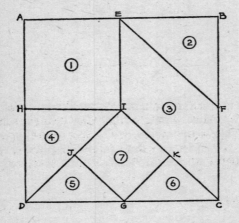

You have now divided your square into seven pieces again, but they are different pieces from your first puzzle. In this puzzle you have made two squares, one bigger than the other; two small triangles which are the same size as each other; two large triangles, the same size as each other and one shape called a parallelogram which has two long sides

60

which are parallel to each other and two short sides which are parallel to each other. A parallelogram looks like a rectangle which has slipped to one side.

Can you use the pieces of this Tangram to make the following geometrical shapes? A rectangle, some more squares, a trapezium? Do you know what a trapezium is? A trapezium is a figure which has four sides, two of which are parallel. These figures are both trapeziums.

Using this Tangram, you can make up some signs which you could use to direct people. Can you make these three arrows?

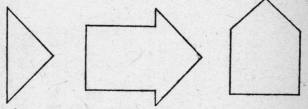

You can also make some interesting shapes which are *symmetrical*. Do you know what that means? It is a shape which is exactly the same on both sides of a central dividing line. Here are some examples of symmetrical shapes which use pieces from your second Tangram. Can you make up some more?

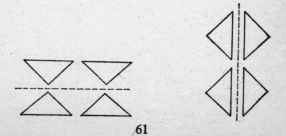

When you are sick in bed you can't always expect a member of the family to come rushing along to your bedside every time you feel like a chat. But if you make a puppet with your hand and a handy handkerchief you will always have someone to talk to whenever you feel like it.

Close your hand, knuckles upwards, so that the top joint of your fingers covers the top joint of your thumbs. Draw a face on your hand with a felt-tip pen. The eyes and nose should be on the side of your hand. Your thumb will make the mouth. Put a handkerchief round your hand to make a headscarf to frame the face.

Now your hand is a puppet and you can make it talk simply by moving your thumb knuckle up and down – and using your own voice to fake the words which the puppet has to say.

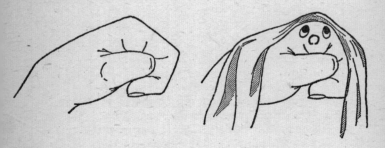

HOW MEANINGS CHANGE

Read these poems through and then read them again, but the second time move the commas and therefore the point at which you pause, back to follow the first noun. Each description now changes, doesn't it?

I saw a Fishpond

I saw a fishpond all on fire,
I saw a house bow to a squire,
I saw a parson twelve feet high,
I saw a cottage near the sky,
I saw a balloon made of lead,
I saw a coffin drop down dead,
I saw two sparrows run a race,
I saw two horses making lace,
I saw a girl just like a cat,
I saw a kitten wear a hat,
I saw a man who saw these too,
And said though strange they all were true.

The first two lines would be read the second time as:

I saw a fishpond, all on fire
I saw a house, bow to a squire
I saw a parson, ...

I saw a Peacock with a Fiery Tail

I saw a Peacock with a fiery tail,
I saw a blazing Comet drop down hail,
I saw a Cloud with ivy circled round,
I saw a sturdy Oak creep on the ground,
I saw a Pismire* swallow up a whale,
I saw a whirling Sea brim full of ale,
I saw a Venice Glass† sixteen foot deep,
I saw a Well full of men's tears that weep,
I saw their Eyes all in a flame of fire,
I saw a House as big as the moon and higher,
I saw the Sun even in the midst of night,
I saw the Man that saw this wondrous sight.

* Pismire = ant
† Venice Glass = coloured glass made on an island in the
Venice lagoon.

Arithmetic

Arithmetic is where numbers fly like pigeons in and out of
   your head.

Arithmetic tells you how many you lose or win if you know
   how many you had before you lost or won.

Arithmetic is seven eleven all good children go to heaven –
   or five six bundle of sticks.

Arithmetic is numbers you squeeze from your head to your
   hand to your pencil to your paper till you get the answer.

Arithmetic is where the answer is right and everything is
   nice and you can look out of the window and see the blue
   sky – or the answer is wrong and you have to start all over
   again and try again and see how it comes out this time.

If you take a number and double it and double it again and
   then double it a few more times, the number gets bigger
   and bigger and goes higher and higher and only arithmetic can tell you what the number is when you decide to
   quit doubling.

Arithmetic is where you have to multiply – and you carry
   the multiplication table in your head and hope you won't
   lose it.

If you have two animal crackers, one good and one bad, and
   you eat one and a striped zebra with streaks all over him
   eats the other, how many animal crackers will you have if
   somebody offers you five six seven and you say No no no
   and you say Nay nay nay and you say Nix nix nix?

If you ask your mother for a fried egg for breakfast and she
   gives you two fried eggs and you eat both of them, who
   is better in arithmetic, you or your mother?

Carl Sandburg

Double It

My husband used to play this game as an only child and he
can still rattle off the doubling table.

   Start with 1, and in your mind double it (2), double it (4),
double it ... Quite soon you'll probably have to take to

paper and add or multiply by 2 to double. If you placed one grain of rice on the first square of a chess board, 2 on the second, 4 on the third and so on, how much rice would the last square hold?

Counting
If you get tired of counting *one, two, three,* make up your own numbers, as shepherds used to do when they had to count sheep day in, day out. You can try using these sets of words instead of numbers when you have to count to ten.

Ounce	Instant	Archery
Dice	Distant	Butchery
Trice	Tryst	Treachery
Quartz	Catalyst	Taproom
Quince	Quest	Tomb
Sago	Sycamore	Sermon
Serpent	Sophomore	Cinnamon
Oxygen	Oculist	Apron
Nitrogen	Novelist	Nunnery
Denim	Dentist	Dennity

Alastair Reid

POCKET CALCULATOR GAMES

Pocket calculators haven't been around very long and certainly not long enough at a price that people can afford. However things are changing and many people use them at work and at school. If you are lucky enough to belong to a family in which someone owns a pocket calculator, and the owner will lend it to you there are lots of games to play and curious sums to work out. You might even be able to save up and buy one for yourself, both to play with and to help you with your arithmetic. Or you may already have one.

First let's have a look at how a calculator works. Some calculators will do such things as converting feet into metres and doing square roots, but most of them are what is known as four-function calculators, which means that you can use them for the four functions of adding, subtracting, multi-plying and dividing.

The face of a four-function calculator looks something like this:

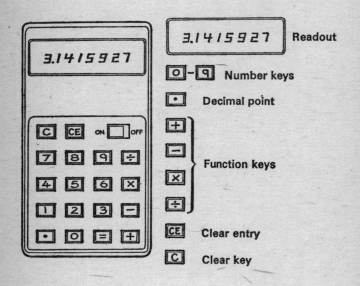

Now to the games – first a couple of easy ones, then some to set you thinking. –

How Old Are We?
Work out the average age of your family by adding all the ages together and dividing by the number of people in the family. Here is an example:

      Mr Popplewell is 35

      Mrs Popplewell is 33

      Catherine Popplewell is 10

      Mark Popplewell is 7

      James Popplewell is 3

So, their total age is 88 years. There are five people in the family so their average age is 17.6 years. That will make the parents feel young and the children feel very grown up, won't it?

Adding

Add groups of one number together as far as the calculator will allow. For instance, add 1, 11, 111, 1111 and so on.

Calculate them out

This game can be played with an ordinary pack of cards, but as it uses your ability with numbers I have included it here and you could work the sums out on the calculator, particularly when you want to make a long run.

Take all the kings, queens and jacks out of the pack. Count the aces as ones. Lay all the cards out in a line on a table or on the floor. (You can lay out a few at a time if you haven't got enough space, but of course you won't be able to clear the lot at once.) The object of the game is to remove all the cards by adding, subtracting, multiplying or dividing the cards next to each other so that they equal the card on their right. You then take all the cards which have made the sum (including the answer card) out of the game and move the line back to fill the space.

Here are some examples to show you how to play.

Using addition

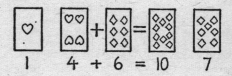

1   4 + 6 = 10   7

67

You can now remove 4, 6, and 10. You then close in the space, so that 1 and 7 are next to each other.

Using subtraction

$$6 \qquad 8 - 1 = 7 \qquad 5$$

Remove 8, 1 and 7. Move 6 and 5 together.

Using multiplication

$$2 \qquad 2 \times 3 = 6 \qquad 5$$

Remove 2, 3 and 6. Move 2 and 5 together.

Using division

$$3 \qquad 10 \div 2 = 5 \qquad 8$$

Take out 10, 2 and 5. Move the 8 and 3 together.

These first examples have shown simple sums using only one function at a time and taking out only three cards each time. But you can mix functions and take out more cards at a time. The real champion will calculate how to take out all forty cards in one fell swoop. Here is a mixed calculation sum.

$$1 + 7 \div 4 \times 5 = 10$$

Here is another one:

$$5 \quad 7 + 4 - 3 = 8 \quad 10$$

Warning: When playing this game, don't leave yourself with only two cards on the table because then you can't get rid of them. Think ahead all the time and take out as many cards as you can in each turn.

999

As you will know this is the number you should dial on the telephone in case of emergency when you want the police, the fire brigade or an ambulance. But for this game your aim is simply to reach 999 as fast as you can on the readout of your calculator. You need two dice as well as the calculator, and you need your wits about you! When you throw the two dice, one will give you the number key to use, the other will tell you the function. Here is a table which decides the value of each function for you:

>   If you throw 1 you add (+)
>   2 you subtract (−)
>   3 you multiply (×)
>   4 you divide (÷)
>   5 you add (+)
>   6 you multiply (×)

It is up to you to decide which dice in each throw you use for the number and which for the function. For example, if you have ten on the readout and then you throw six and two, you could either use two for the function and subtract six, or you could multiply ten by two and reach twenty.

You have to reach exactly 999 in the fewest possible turns. If you go over 999, you have to work back towards it, using the divide and subtract function as often as you can. But sometimes it's worth subtracting or dividing earlier in the game to give yourself a better number to work from. That's where the wit and number skill comes in!

Wipe the readout out
This is a game for someone who really has a feeling for numbers, but it is also a game which can strengthen your number sense. The aim of the game is to start with any six digit number on the readout (a number with six numbers or digits in it, like 256893) and try to work down to 0 on the readout in four turns.

At first you may be tempted to divide early in the game, but unless you have a suitable number to divide into you will find you have decimal numbers which are very difficult to get rid of. For example, if you divided 256893 by 200 to begin with you would get 1284.465, but if you subtracted 93 first and then divided by 200, you would get 1284, a much better figure to work with.

There are three essential rules in this game. You cannot multiply or divide by 0, which would of course give you 0 straight away, nor can you subtract the whole number on the readout. Once you have 'played' a number, you can't wipe it out. The real skill in this game is the ability to *estimate*, that is to make an accurate guess at the number which is most likely to give you the answer you want. This is probably the most important of all mathematical skills.

Draw this board on a piece of paper. Using the numbers from 1 to 9 only, write them in the squares so that each lines across, down and diagonally adds up to 15. On page 96 you will find a couple of solutions to this problem.

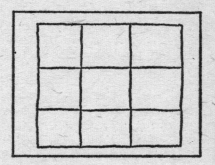

Yet another version of this game is the magic circle. Draw a wheel of ten circles round a central circle. Join the outer circles with spokes to the centre as shown here.

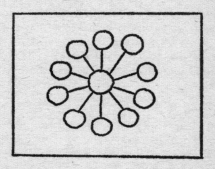

Now write the numbers 1 to 11 in the circles so that the sum of any three numbers across the circle in a straight line adds up to the sum of every other set of circles in a straight line. It can be done! The solution is on page 96.

At Your Desk

A diary is by its nature a very private thing that you usually only do by yourself, even if one day you let someone else read it. You should, of course, never read anyone else's diary unless you have permission.

Traditionally one starts a diary on New Year's Day and makes an entry every day. In fact many people do start a diary on New Year's Day and keep it for a month or two and then when they find they are just writing things like, 'Went to school. Mincemeat for dinner. Watched television,' they stop. But you can start a diary any time you want and you can use it many different ways. Here are a few ideas.

A Five Year Diary
You can buy one or you can make your own with a big exercise book. Each page is divided into five sections and, as you write your entry for the second and following years, you can see above what you were doing exactly a year ago. I don't think I managed to keep mine for as long as five years but it certainly had entries for the whole of the first three years.

A Day Book
For this you need a notebook or looseleaf folder rather than any of the diaries you can buy in the shops, because you want to be able to write as little or as much as you want and you may not want to write on every day of the year.

In a day book you need not just write what *happened* each day, you can write your thoughts and feelings or put in a poem or a picture, a joke or a quotation or paste in something which will remind you of that moment in your life.

In a day book you might make several entries one month and only one or two in another. You don't therefore have that awful sense of discouragement known to many a formal diary keeper when they have forgotten to make an entry for several days or really have nothing much to say.

Entries in a day book might go something like this:

1st January 19 . . The first day of the year and the first day of my day book. We went to the pantomime. Here is the programme.

2nd January It snowed last night and today we went walking in the woods. No one had been there before us. Our feet fell quietly on the snow-covered fallen leaves. We saw a squirrel and the tracks of a hare. In the afternoon the snow had all melted except in a few corners.

5th January I read this poem today and I want to keep it in my book so I will remember it.

Upon the Snail

She goes but softly, but she goeth sure;
    She stumbles not as stronger creatures do:
Her journey's shorter, so she may endure
    Better than they which do much further go.

She makes no noise, but stilly seizeth on
    The flower or herb appointed for her food,
The which she quietly doth feed upon,
    While others range, and glare, but find no good.

And though she doth but softly go,
    However 'tis not fast, nor slow, but sure;
And certainly they that do travel so,
    The prize they do aim at, they do procure.

                          John Bunyan

7th January Back to school today. Margaret has a new fur hat and a good joke. 'What is brown and dangerous?' 'A man-eating mole.' We had art and I painted this picture of our walk in the woods last week.

11th February Today is my birthday. This is my favourite card. It is still very cold, but the evenings are at last really beginning to get lighter. My mother's evening class put on a play last week. Here is a picture of it which appeared in the paper, and a copy of the programme. Father thought it was very funny and laughed very loudly which embarrassed me rather.

A Nature Diary

This could be combined with a day book like the one described above or could be a quite separate activity. Again it is probably best not to buy a diary but to use an exercise book or looseleaf folder. Divide each page into three or more columns and give each a heading. The first should be for the date. The other could be Weather, Growing Things. Animals and Birds, the Night Sky or any other topic you are interested in. Try to make an entry in at least one column every day.

Here is what a page in your nature diary might look like:

Have you ever thought of having a pen friend in another country? Some people get a pen friend because they are learning a language and want to use it and perhaps one day visit that country. Other people choose a pen friend because they want to learn about another country. You can also be helping another person who is trying to learn English.

How do you go about getting a pen friend? If you are learning a language at school, your teacher may be able to put you in touch with an organization or school to whom you can write. Alternatively you could write direct to one of these organizations which will put you in touch with someone in the country of your choice.

International Friendship League, Peacehaven Hostel, Creswich Road, London W3, 01-992-0221.

International Scholastic Correspondence, Dovenden, Tipton St John, Sidmouth, Devon.

But remember that having a pen friend is not something you should take on too lightly. If you are going to tell someone that you want to write to them and become their friend, you must keep it up and write regularly. Just think how disappointed you would be if you had a pen friend who didn't write to *you*.

What should you say in your first letter? Well, what would you want to know about a new friend? Your letter should be friendly and tell your new friend how old you are, who the members of your family are (including any pets which you may write about sometimes), what sort of place you live in, what sort of school you go to and what subjects you like at school, what hobbies or special interests you have, what work your parents do. Later you could write in more detail about the area in which you live. You could also ask questions in your letters to show your pen friend the sort of things you would like to know about his or her country.

Once the correspondence gets going you should have no difficulty finding things to talk about.

ENLARGING AND REDUCING

Have you ever tried to copy a picture or a map? It is much easier to do if you use squared paper. It is even easy to enlarge the picture and make it much bigger or reduce the picture and make it much smaller. Take the original picture and, if you can't write on the page it is on (as you probably cannot or you would use the original picture), lay a sheet of thin tracing paper over it. Now draw vertical and horizontal lines 1.5 cm ($\frac{1}{2}$ in) apart so that the whole picture is covered by a grid of squares. (If it is a very big picture or map you are reducing, then you might use larger squares.)

Now take the piece of paper on to which you want to copy the picture. Draw a grid of squares on to that. If you want the picture the same size, then make the squares the same size. If you want the new picture to be larger, then make the squares larger. If you want the new picture to be smaller, then make smaller squares.

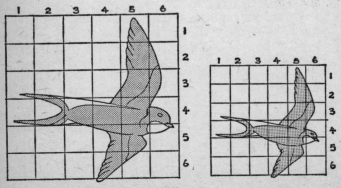

Now copy the picture square by square on to the blank grid. It may help you if you number the squares along the top and down the side as shown. You can then check that you are copying the correct square!

THE WHAT-DO-YOU-KNOW TREASURE HUNT

Find out as much as you can about the following things in one afternoon or in one week-end. Use your local library, your own books, encyclopedia or any other source of information. Ask other people. Is there anything about these subjects on television or radio during this time when you're having your treasure hunt?

stegosaurus
treasure trove
tuber
papier-mâché
sycamore
chronometers

molluscs
heraldry
chinook
glass blowing
pomegranates
sea anemones

If you have enjoyed doing this, show this first list to an adult and ask them to give you another list to work from on another occasion.

On a Journey

From *A Railway Carriage*

Faster than fairies, faster than witches,
Bridges and houses, hedges and ditches;
And charging along like troops in a battle,
All through the meadows the horses and cattle:
All the sights of the hill and the plain
Fly as thick as driving rain;
And ever again in the wink of an eye,
Painted stations whistle by.

Here is a child who clambers and scrambles,
All by himself and gathering brambles;
Here is a tramp who stands and gazes;
And there is the green for stringing daisies.
Here is a cart run away in the road
Lumping along with man and load;
And here is a mill and there is a river.
Each a glimpse and gone for ever!

Robert Louis Stevenson

WHERE DO THEY COME FROM?

When a car is being driven in a foreign country where it is
not licensed, it is usual for it to have a disc on with a letter or
letters to show where it has come from. Here is a list of these
international plaques. See how many of them you can see
and collect as you are travelling around.

A	Austria	IR	Iran
AUS	Australia	IRQ	Iraq
B	Belgium	J	Japan
BG	Bulgaria	L	Luxembourg
CDN	Canada	RL	Lebanon
CH	Switzerland	MA	Morocco
CL	Ceylon (now Sri Lanka)	MC	Monaco
CS	Czechoslovakia	N	Norway
CY	Cyprus	NL	Holland (Netherlands)
D	Germany (Deutschland)	NZ	New Zealand
DK	Denmark	P	Portugal
E	Spain (Espagne)	PAK	Pakistan
IRL	Eire (Ireland)	PL	Poland
ET	Egypt	R	Rumania
F	France	S	Sweden
GB	Great Britain	SF	Finland (Suomi)
GBZ	Gibraltar	SU	USSR (Soviet Union)
GH	Ghana	TN	Tunisia
GR	Greece	TR	Turkey
H	Hungary	USA	United States of America
I	Italy		
IL	Israel	WAN	Nigeria (in West Africa)
IND	India	YU	Yugoslavia

I SAW IT

Make a list of things which you might see on your journey.
Tick them off as you see them. Can you find them all before
the end of the journey?

Here is a list for a journey by car or train:

    a large black dog
    a level crossing
    a policeman
    a market
    a milkman
    a baby
    a school

an oak tree

a hospital

a playground

When travelling by air you often seem to spend almost as much time sitting around waiting for the aeroplane as you do flying. Here is a list of things to watch for when waiting in an airport:

a pilot

an air hostess

a porter

a cleaner

an advertisement for car hire

a person speaking a foreign language

a man with a waistcoat

a baby

a lady wearing red

a large parcel

COLLECTING THE ALPHABET

See if you can see an object beginning with each letter of the alphabet. Collect them in order from A to Z during your journey. You can skip really difficult letters like O, U, V, X, Y and Z if they hold you up too long.

Here is a specimen list from one journey: Aeroplane, Bus, Cat, Dog, Entry sign, Field, Gravel drive, House, Indian lady, Jacket, Kennel, Lorry, Man, Nest, Oak tree, Pavement, Q (skipped), Roundabout, Shop, Tanker lorry, U, V (skipped,) Woman, X (skipped), Yoyo, Z (gave up!).

If you were on an aeroplane you could make up a list of animals, places or action words (verbs, like acting, balancing, crawling).

Another, rather more difficult, version of this game is to look for words *ending* with each letter of the alphabet. It is probably best not to do this in order from A to Z but to make a list of the letters and then to check them off when you sight an object. You will probably have to bar I, J, Q, U, V, X and Z, but give yourself a double mark if you manage to get them! Your list might start like this: TraiN, treE, boY, gulL, clouD, riveR, leaving A, B, C, F, G, H (I), (J), K, M, (O), P, (Q), S, T, (U), V, W, (X) and (Z) to be found.

CAR NUMBERS

This is a game that can be played every time you are near a road and every time you travel. As a student I used to play a 'round' on my daily way to college quite often. The aim is simply to collect single car numbers in order from 1 to 10 (for the unambitious) and 1–100 (for the ambitious). You start by looking for 1, then 2 and so on up to your target.

FOLLOW THE MAP

Always try to have a map with you and trace where you are going. Watch out for the towns and villages, any rivers or road junctions you cross. Does your map show places of special interest like churches, windmills, woods, hills, railway lines and so on? Watch out for the real thing as you pass it.

Making Things

BREWING GINGER BEER

You can set up your own ginger beer brewery and have fresh new ginger beer all through the summer.

You will need:
    3 teaspoons ground ginger
    200 g ($\frac{1}{2}$ lb) sugar
    $\frac{1}{2}$ tsp cream of tartar
    the juice and rind of one lemon
    $2\frac{1}{4}$ l (4 pints) boiling water
    12 g ($\frac{1}{2}$ oz) dried yeast

1 Mix together in a large container the ginger, sugar, cream of tartar and the rind from the lemon.
2 Pour on the boiling water. Stir the mixture until the sugar has dissolved.
3 Leave the mixture to stand until it has cooled but is still warm.
4 Stir in the yeast and the juice from the lemon.
5 Cover the container and leave the beer for 24 hours.
6 Now skim off the yeast which has risen to the top. Strain the remaining liquid into a jug and pour it into bottles.
7 Put the lids on the bottles and let the ginger beer 'rest' for three days before drinking. Drink within the next week or it will ferment.

October 31st is All Hallows Eve or Hallowe'en when spirits are supposed to rise from their graves to wander the world. At one time young people used to get together to try to divine the future, and often frighten themselves into a state of terror in so doing. Now Hallowe'en is sometimes seen as an excuse for a party with games and merriment. At Hallowe'en the decorations are witches and ghosts and symbols of magic. When I was young we always used to make a jack-o-lantern out of a big pumpkin and stand it in the window to look out into the night with a grim grin.

Pumpkins are quite cheap to buy. You will also need a candle or nightlight, a sharp knife and a strong kitchen spoon.

Cut the top off the pumpkin and put it to one side. With the knife, mark eyes, nose and mouth (with splaying teeth) on to the pumpkin. Then, using the knife to cut and the spoon to gouge out, hollow the centre of the pumpkin. Throw away the seeds, but you could use the rest of the fruit to make pumpkin pie. When you have cut out enough of the centre to make the walls of pumpkin skin about 1.5 cm ($\frac{1}{2}$ in) thick, cut the features out through to the inside. Stand your candle firmly inside the pumpkin. Put the top back on again as a lid and check that it is not too near the candle. When night falls, light the candle, close the top and put your jack-o-lantern on the windowsill to appear as a ghostly face to those outside.

When Christmas comes you may have lots of friends and relations to send Christmas cards. And your family might like you to make the cards for them to send out, too. If you only have to make a few cards, you can make each one individually, but if you have a large number to make you may want to choose a design which will allow you to use an 'assembly line' method. To do this you need a design for which you can cut out a number of pieces at once, paint or decorate them all at the same time and then put them together. If you can break the work down into stages and do each stage a large number of times, you can produce more cards more quickly and more effectively.

Here are some ideas to use for this assembly line method.

Christmas tree cards

You need: Base cards, green paper, red paper, a packet of silver and/or gold stars, scissors, glue, pencil. Draw a pattern of a Christmas tree and its pot on card. Cut out the tree in several layers of green paper. Take care not to use thick paper for this; tissue paper would be fine. Cut out the pot in several layers of red paper. Stick the trees and pots onto the base cards. Decorate the trees with the stick on stars. Write your message inside.

Father Christmas cards

You need: Red card, pink paper, cotton wool, scissors, glue, pen. Cut out triangles of red card. Cut out circles of pink paper for the face.

Stick the face onto the triangle. Stick on a scrap of cotton wool for a beard. Draw in a face and you have your Father Christmas card. Write your message on the back.

Candle cards

You need: Base cards, white paper, green paper, red, orange and yellow tissue paper, scissors, pencil, glue. Cut thin rectangles of white paper, for the candles. Cut slivers of tissue paper, for the candle flame. Cut holly leaf shapes in green paper. Cut the white paper candle and stick it on the backing card. Make a 'flickering' tissue paper flame. Put holly leaves around the base of the candle. Write your message on the back or inside the card.

JIGSAW PUZZLES

Whenever I do a jigsaw, someone always seems to come along and watch over my shoulder and find all the pieces I am looking for before I do. Despite this, jigsaws are a wonderful pastime. The ones I like best are those with pictures of famous paintings so that you really get to know the details of the picture while you are putting the puzzle together.

Have you ever tried making your own jigsaw puzzle? One of the great advantages of this is that you can keep the puzzle in an envelope and take it with you on holiday or on a journey.

Take a picture from a magazine and stick it on a piece

of thin card. Smooth it down carefully and let the glue dry thoroughly. Then cut the card into irregular-shaped pieces.

Mix the pieces up and then see how quickly you can put the picture together again.

You could cut up a picture postcard (without backing it) to make a very small jigsaw. You could also make an amusing birthday card or get-well card for a friend by designing the card on light cardboard and then cutting it up like a jigsaw and putting it into the envelope so that your friend has to put the pieces together in order to get the message.

Have you ever made a scrapbook? We have one in which we stick postcards of the places we have been with the dates when we were there. We have also made holiday scrapbooks with postcards, maps, pressed flowers, tickets and drawings and photographs of the places we have been. Sometimes when we have been abroad we have made a scrapbook about the place we were going to before we set out, so we would know more about it. Then we've collected extra things to complete it when we came back. We've also made a scrapbook of autumn leaves and seeds, pressing and drying them before we pasted them in and labelled them.

Here are some more ideas for making a scrapbook which might set you off to making one of your own.

Transport – showing the development of different forms of transport throughout the ages. Cut pictures from magazines and copy drawings from books. Write in some information about where and when the transport was used and how it worked. Don't just stick to motorized transport. Think of things like dog sledges, bullock carts and camels too.

Fashion – a pageant of clothes through the ages. Find a book in the library to help you with this. See if you can find out what the different bits of clothing were called and label your pictures. Write in the dates to show when the clothes were in fashion.

See if you can find out what the following were or are:
a bustle a cardinal a mantle a mob cap a dolman an Inverness cape a farthingale a toga a frock coat a surcoat a mule a furbelow a Glengarry bonnet trews a reticule a stomacher bloomers a kirtle a wimple a chaplet a doublet a jerkin a shako

A country alphabet Choose a country for each letter of the alphabet (say, Australia, Belgium, Canada, Denmark, England, France, Germany, Holland, Israel, Japan, Kuwait, Lesotho, Mauritius or Mexico, Nigeria, Outer Mongolia,

Portugal, Qatar, Russia, Spain, Tanzania, Uruguay, Vene-
zuela, Wales [there is no X so you can use this for any other
country you wish], Yugoslavia and Zambia.) Draw a small
map for each page showing the position and shape of the
country in its continent. Find pictures which show the appearance of the land and its people for each country. See if
you know people who could give you a postage stamp for
each country. And see if you can find out some information
about each country and present it in a small panel, like this:

> Tanzania
> Capital: Dar es Salaam
> Population:
> Main produce:
> Climate:

You may find some countries easier to get information
about than others so that some pages will be fuller than
others, but the search is part of the fun.

My football team If you are a football fan it is great fun to
make a scrapbook about your team with pictures of the
players and a little bit of information about them: a record
of the games they play, copies of the programmes of any
games you manage to go to. You might even be able to write
and ask for the team's autographs for your book.

Experimenting

TAKE A BAG OF BALLOONS

You can get a great deal of fun out of a bag of balloons, particularly if they are mixed in shape and size. I hope you don't get too many blue ones in your bag. They always seem to be much harder to blow up than the other colours!

Here are some ideas to start you off:

1 Blow up a balloon. Tie a knot in the neck so that the air won't escape. Throw it in the air – and then try to keep it there. How long can you keep it up without it falling to the ground or touching the furniture? Try keeping it up without touching it with your hands.

2 Blow up a balloon but don't tie it up. Hold it up above your head and then let go. What does it do? How far did it go? Do round balloons do different things from sausage-shaped balloons? Do big balloons behave differently from small balloons? Do they behave differently if you put less air into them?

3 Write your name on a balloon with felt-tip pen or biro. Now blow up the balloon. What happens? Now write your name on the balloon while it is blown up. Let all the air out and see what happens.

4 Play with a balloon outside on a windy day.

5 Juggle with three or more balloons, trying to keep them all in the air at once.

6 Take a balloon and rub it against your body, particularly against any wool you are wearing. Put the balloon against the wall. And it will stay there! The rubbing will have given the balloon a charge of electricity which attracts it to another surface.

The Bird in the Cage

In this picture you see a bird cage and, outside it, a bird. Can you put the bird into the cage?

Take a piece of card and hold it between the bird and the cage, upright on the paper. Put your face against the edge of the card so that one eye can only see the bird and the other eye can only see the cage. Look at them closely for a short time. Gradually the bird will appear to move until it is inside the cage!

Hole in your hand

Roll up a piece of paper so that it makes a tube. Hold the tube up to one eye and hold your hand up to the other eye. Look straight ahead with both eyes at a picture on the wall or at the window. Gradually it will seem that you are looking at the picture through a hole in your hand.

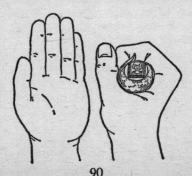

Have you noticed how indoor plants on a windowsill will turn towards the light? Have you ever turned one of them so that the flowers face into the room and watched over a couple of days to see how they turn back to the light from the window?

A sprouting potato will give you a very interesting display of its growth towards the light. Take a small cardboard box like a shoe box. (Shoe shops are usually pleased to get rid of their old shoe boxes. Grocers and sweet shops also have boxes they have to get rid of.) Build some barriers in it with doorways in them, as shown in this picture.

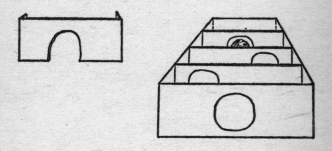

Cut another doorway at one end of the box. Put a sprouting potato in the innermost 'room'. Put the lid back on the box. Place the box in a warm place where the light can shine into the 'doorway' in the outer wall. Leave the box for a couple of days and then start opening it daily to see how the potato sprout is growing.

You can write your name on a plant when it is young and it will grow bigger with the plant. This is how you do it.

On a vegetable marrow you can cut your initials or name out with a sharp knife, but you must take great care to cut only through the outer skin and not into the flesh.

You can also mark a red apple with your name, so it looks as if it's grown there. You will need some insulating tape sufficiently weatherproof to stay on the apple as it grows. Cut your initials out of the tape and stick them on to the apple while it is still green but fully grown. As it ripens from green to red in the sunshine, your initials under the tape will remain green. When you peel off the tape your name will be written on the apple.

Growing a giant vegetable marrow
The size of a vegetable marrow depends a great deal upon how much food and liquid it absorbs as it grows. You can help it along.

When your marrow is half grown, take a large darning needle. Stick it through the fleshy part of the of the stem near the marrow. Thread wool on to the needle and pull it through the stem. Place the end of the wool in a bowl of water and the water will pass up the wool directly into the marrow. Top up the water as the marrow absorbs it or it evaporates. If you add some liquid plant food like Baby Bio to the water this will feed the marrow further. You could mark your name on your giant marrow and see how large it grows.

PINHOLE MICROSCOPES

We read in books, and people tell us, that there are things so small that our eyes cannot see them. Usually we take this on trust, but if you have a microscope you can find out for yourself. A real microscope costs a lot of money, but you can make a very simple microscope which will magnify up to 150 times with very simple materials.

The Magnifying Pinhole
For the simplest microscope of all you only need a piece of dark card and a fine needle! If you have no dark card, paint a piece of white card with black paint. Make a hole in the centre of the card with the needle. Hold up the card and look through the hole at a small object held about an inch away from the hole. You will see it magnified about 10 times!

An interesting experiment can follow from this. After you have looked through the pinhole, remove the card, leaving the object in the same position. You won't be able to see it at all! Why? Because the eye cannot discover a single object which is held so close to it.

Strangely enough, if you look at an object a long way away through the pinhole it will appear smaller than if you look at it with the naked eye. Why?

Waterdrop Microscope

This is a good home-made microscope but you need a sheet of metal, which is not so easy to come by. If you can find one, it's worth it. Bore a hole in the centre of it. What you use for this will depend upon the thickness of your metal plate. Wipe a thin layer of vaseline around the hole you have made, making sure that none of it covers the hole. Using your finger, put a drop of water into the hole, so that it sits like the lens in a magnifying glass. Place any object you want to examine, like a leaf or a feather or a hair from your dog or your own head on a piece of paper. Look through the water drop at it. You will see the object magnified about 150 times!

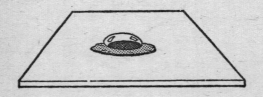

Solutions

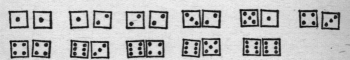

Note: this is one way in which you might throw the sequence. Only 1 + 1, 6 + 5 and 6 + 6 need be the same in every game.

PENNY PUZZLES (p. 44)

1.

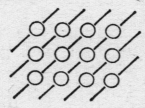

2. *Pass the goats*

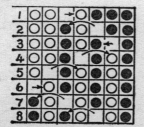

ALPHABETICAL ORDER (p. 47)

1. Tea, telephone, television, temperature, ten, test, thermometer, time, together, top, tray, twenty.
2. Mackerel, magazine, many, mark, mask, measles, meat, meringue, milk, money, more, most, mumps.

PUT IT TOGETHER AGAIN (p. 56)

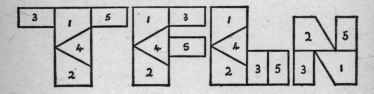

MAGIC SQUARES (p. 71)

8	1	6
3	5	7
4	9	2

2	9	4
7	5	3
6	1	8

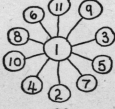